Instant Oracle GoldenGate

A concise and clear step-by-step guide to get
you quickly started with Oracle GoldenGate

Tony Bruzzese

PUBLISHING

BIRMINGHAM - MUMBAI

Instant Oracle GoldenGate

First published: July 2013

Production Reference: 1160713

Published by Packt Publishing Ltd.
Livery Place
35 Livery Street
Birmingham B3 2PB, UK.

ISBN 978-1-78217-024-2

www.packtpub.com

Credits

Author
Tony Bruzzese

Reviewer
Satishbabu Gunukula

Acquisition Editor
Kevin Colaco

Commissioning Editor
Yogesh Dalvi

Technical Editor
Sonali S. Vernekar

Project Coordinator
Sherin Padayatty

Proofreader
Stephen Copestake

Production Coordinator
Conidon Miranda

Cover Work
Conidon Miranda

About the Author

Tony Bruzzese is a seasoned Oracle and Unix practitioner with more than 20 years of experience in architecting, troubleshooting, optimizing, and maximizing large scale clusters, highly complex systems using Oracle, UNIX, and third party technologies. He has worked in the Telecom Industry at Bell Canada, moved on to a consulting firm at CGI, and more recently in the BlackBerry Manufacturing arm of BlackBerry. Now a freelance IT consultant, he specializes in helping customers to resolve Oracle performance problems, designing disaster recovery for Oracle databases, implementing high availability solutions, and general database architecting. Tony's consulting endeavors are usually brief because he diagnoses and fixes problems quickly, generally in a few days. Tony is also Oracle 11g certified (OCP) and has maintained his certifications since Oracle 8.0.

About the Reviewer

Satishbabu Gunukula has over 13 years of experience in the IT Industry. He has extensive experience in Oracle and SQLServer Database Technologies and specializes in high availability solutions such as Oracle RAC, Data Guard, Grid Control, and SQLServer Cluster. He has done Master's degree in Computer Applications.

Satishbabu Gunukula has been honored with the prestigious Oracle ACE Award. He has experience on and wide range of products such as Essbase, Hyperion, Agile, SAP Basis, MySQL, Linux, Windows, and Business Apps administration, and he has implemented many business critical systems for fortune 500, 1000 companies.

He reviews articles for SELECT Journal – the publication of IOUG-and also books for Packt Publishing. He is an active member in IOUG, Oracle RAC SIG, UKOUG, and OOW. He has written articles for major publications and websites and spoken at Oracle-related events. He shares knowledge on his websites http://www.oracleracexpert.com and http://www.sqlserver-expert.com.

www.PacktPub.com

Support files, eBooks, discount offers, and more

You might want to visit www.PacktPub.com for support files and downloads related to your book.

Did you know that Packt offers eBook versions of every book published, with PDF and ePub files available? You can upgrade to the eBook version at www.PacktPub.com and as a print book customer, you are entitled to a discount on the eBook copy. Get in touch with us at service@packtpub.com for more details.

At www.PacktPub.com, you can also read a collection of free technical articles, sign up for a range of free newsletters and receive exclusive discounts and offers on Packt books and eBooks.

http://PacktLib.PacktPub.com

Do you need instant solutions to your IT questions? PacktLib is Packt's online digital book library. Here, you can access, read and search across Packt's entire library of books.

Why Subscribe?

► Fully searchable across every book published by Packt

► Copy-and-paste, print and bookmark content

► On demand and accessible via web browser

Free Access for Packt account holders

If you have an account with Packt at www.PacktPub.com, you can use this to access PacktLib today and view nine entirely free books. Simply use your login credentials for immediate access.

Instant Updates on New Packt Books

Get notified! Find out when new books are published by following @PacktEnterprise on Twitter, or the *Packt Enterprise* Facebook page.

Table of Contents

Preface

Data duplication is ubiquitous in enterprises today. Almost every application in an organization needs information from some other part of the organization. Oracle GoldenGate has become such a predominant tool in the industry today thus allowing organizations to share data between disparate environments. Its adoption rate is increasing very quickly because of the ease of use, economy of speed, and small footprint required to implement it.

What this book covers

Implementing design considerations (Simple) presents a number of design decisions to consider, such as your platform of choice, physical memory requirements, storage, and network considerations such as high and low latency networks.

Installing Oracle GoldenGate (Simple) guides you through the step-by-step process of downloading the software from Oracle's website, unpacking the software, and installing it on your server host.

Creating one-way replication (Simple) will explore how to implement a downstream replication by creating Extract and Pump processes on the source system for capturing and transporting source data to your target system. A Replicat process is created on your target server which applies changes received from the source system.

Creating bidirectional replication (Simple) also sometimes referred to as master to master replication, performs the same steps as in the recipe, *Creating one-way replication (Simple)* and in the opposite direction.

Creating heterogeneous replication (Simple) lets you start discovering the ease of implementing replication between disparate RDBMS environments, such as Oracle to SQL Server. However, there are a number of other different RDBMS combinations as well.

Configuring Oracle GoldenGate for High Availability (HA) (Simple) although might sound more complex than it really is, it is quite simple and differs slightly from a single-instance installation.

Configuring advanced settings (Simple) discovers the power and flexibility of Oracle GoldenGate to perform tasks such as data mapping, filtering, and data transformation.

Performing encryption in OGG (Simple) discusses encrypting the Oracle GoldenGate user ID and trail files at rest and in flight using Blowfish and AES algorithms for 128, 192, and 256 bits.

Managing Oracle GoldenGate (Simple) allows you to explore some of the more interactive commands to view, monitor, and troubleshoot Oracle GoldenGate processes during a running instance.

Performance tuning (Simple) explores plausible solutions to increase efficiencies and data throughput in your environment, even under high latency networks, as one of the most common concerns regarding replication is how to get data faster to the target system.

What you need for this book

In order to use Oracle GoldenGate, you need an existing Oracle database in place, or any of the supported databases for Oracle GoldenGate such as SQL Server, Teradata, Sybase, and so on. Then, and only then, you can download and use the Oracle GoldenGate software. For a complete list of supported database, you can reference Oracle® GoldenGate Windows and Unix Administrator's Guide 11g Release 2 Patch Set 1 (11.2.1.0.1) E29397-01.

Who this book is for

Typically, Oracle GoldenGate is administered by database administrators because its design is database-centric. Although, not limited to database administrators, data specialists, data architects can also make use of the product from a quality assurance perspective.

Conventions

In this book, you will find a number of styles of text that distinguish between different kinds of information. Here are some examples of these styles, and an explanation of their meaning:

Code words in text are shown as follows: "We can include other contexts through the use of the `include` directive."

A block of code is set as follows:

```
OGG_SRVC =
(DESCRIPTION =
    (ADDRESS = (PROTOCOL = TCP)(HOST = hosta1-vip)(PORT = 1521))
    (ADDRESS = (PROTOCOL = TCP)(HOST = hosta2-vip)(PORT = 1521))
    (LOAD_BALANCE = NO)
    (CONNECT_DATA =
```

```
                (SERVER = DEDICATED)
                (SERVICE_NAME = OGG_SRVC)
        )
    )
```

When we wish to draw your attention to a particular part of a code block, the relevant lines or items are set in bold:

SPECIALRUN

  ENDRUN

  SETENV (ORACLE_SID="TRG101")

  SETENV (ORACLE_HOME="/u01/app/oracle/product/11.2.0/db_1")

  SETENV (NLS_LANG = "AMERICAN_AMERICA.AL32UTF8")

Any command-line input or output is written as follows:

```
$ ln -s /ggtrail/dirdat    /GG/dirdat
$ ln -s /ggtrail/dirchk    /GG/dirchk
$ ln -s /ggtrail/br        /GG/br
$ ln -s /ggtrail/dirtmp    /GG/dirtmp
```

New terms and **important words** are shown in bold. Words that you see on the screen, in menus or dialog boxes for example, appear in the text like this: "clicking the **Next** button moves you to the next screen".

 Warnings or important notes appear in a box like this.

Reader feedback

Feedback from our readers is always welcome. Let us know what you think about this book—what you liked or may have disliked. Reader feedback is important for us to develop titles that you really get the most out of.

To send us general feedback, simply send an e-mail to feedback@packtpub.com, and mention the book title via the subject of your message.

If there is a topic that you have expertise in and you are interested in either writing or contributing to a book, see our author guide on www.packtpub.com/authors.

Customer support

Now that you are the proud owner of a Packt book, we have a number of things to help you to get the most from your purchase.

Errata

Although we have taken every care to ensure the accuracy of our content, mistakes do happen. If you find a mistake in one of our books—maybe a mistake in the text or the code—we would be grateful if you would report this to us. By doing so, you can save other readers from frustration and help us improve subsequent versions of this book. If you find any errata, please report them by visiting http://www.packtpub.com/submit-errata, selecting your book, clicking on the **errata submission form** link, and entering the details of your errata. Once your errata are verified, your submission will be accepted and the errata will be uploaded on our website, or added to any list of existing errata, under the Errata section of that title. Any existing errata can be viewed by selecting your title from http://www.packtpub.com/support.

Piracy

Piracy of copyright material on the Internet is an ongoing problem across all media. At Packt, we take the protection of our copyright and licenses very seriously. If you come across any illegal copies of our works, in any form, on the Internet, please provide us with the location address or website name immediately so that we can pursue a remedy.

Please contact us at copyright@packtpub.com with a link to the suspected pirated material.

We appreciate your help in protecting our authors, and our ability to bring you valuable content.

Questions

You can contact us at questions@packtpub.com if you are having a problem with any aspect of the book, and we will do our best to address it.

Instant Oracle GoldenGate

Welcome to Instant Oracle GoldenGate. In the following recipes you'll be exploring Oracle GoldenGate in a succession of building concepts; from understanding the required components of Oracle GoldenGate, to simple replication, and onto more complex configurations and advanced topics. The purpose of this book is to get you up-and-running with as little effort as possible by getting down to the essential building blocks of replication.

Implementing design considerations (Simple)

In this recipe, we'll be discussing some of the fundamental design components that you need to understand when planning to use **Oracle GoldenGate** (**OGG**) in your existing enterprise. We'll be discussing in some detail the various infrastructure requirements in order to support OGG in the organization.

How to do it...

In order to support your GoldenGate installation, you must ensure you have ample physical memory (RAM) available on the server. The steps for implementing the design considerations are as follows:

1. The following command will display your available memory on the server:

   ```
   $ /usr/sbin/lsattr -El sys0 -a realmmem
   ```

The output of the preceding command will be as follows:

```
Realmem 16777216 Amount of usable physical memory in Kbytes False
```

The preceding output indicates that the server has 16 GB of physical RAM, which is more than sufficient to carry on for an **Online Transaction Processing** (**OLTP**) environment.

2. For very busy systems, you can limit the amount of RAM to your Extract and/or Replicat processes as in the following parameter file:

```
cachemgr cachesize 8G
```

3. Your OGG software distribution should have its own filesystem created by your system administrator. Our example is a 100 GB filesystem.

```
hosta> $ df -g
```

The output of the preceding command will be as follows:

```
Filesystem      GB blocks       Free  %  Used      Iused   %Iused
Mounted on

...

/dev/oggvg          100.00         99.67      1%          270
1%     /u01/app/oracle/GG
```

4. Next we want to calculate the optimal network bandwidth in order to set the TCP Send / Receive socket buffers (TCPBUFSIZE) for data pump extracts. Use the following command to get the correct TCPBUFSIZE buffers for your data pump extract:

```
hosta> $ ping -c 10 hostb
```

The output of the preceding command will be as follows:

```
PING hostb: (10.3.4.5): 56 data bytes
64 bytes from 10.3.4.5: icmp_seq=0 ttl=255 time=0.8 ms
64 bytes from 10.3.4.5: icmp_seq=1 ttl=255 time=0.8 ms
64 bytes from 10.3.4.5: icmp_seq=2 ttl=255 time=0.8 ms
64 bytes from 10.3.4.5: icmp_seq=3 ttl=255 time=0.8 ms
64 bytes from 10.3.4.5: icmp_seq=4 ttl=255 time=0.8 ms
64 bytes from 10.3.4.5: icmp_seq=5 ttl=255 time=0.8 ms
64 bytes from 10.3.4.5: icmp_seq=6 ttl=255 time=0.8 ms
64 bytes from 10.3.4.5: icmp_seq=7 ttl=255 time=0.7 ms
64 bytes from 10.3.4.5: icmp_seq=8 ttl=255 time=0.8 ms
```

```
64 bytes from 10.3.4.5: icmp_seq=9 ttl=255 time=0.8 ms


----hostb PING Statistics----

10 packets transmitted, 10 packets received, 0% packet loss

round-trip min/avg/max = 0.8/0.8/0.8 ms
```

Now we'll calculate the buffer size based on the preceding output of 0.8 ms network latency and our 100 megabits interface card. You might have a different speed interface card such as 1 gigabit or even 10 gigabits. Check with your system administrator if you're unsure.

0.8 seconds * 100 megabits per second = 8 megabits

To determine the buffer size in bytes, where 8 bits = 1 byte, we perform the following calculation:

8 megabits / 8 = 1,000,000 bytes ~ 1 MB / second = TCPBUFSIZE

5. Create an Oracle service for OGG to connect to the Oracle database via a service name in a high availability **Real Application Clusters** (**RAC**) database as follows:

```
$ srvctl add service -d sourcedb -s OGG_SRVC -r hosta1 -a hosta2
$ srvctl start service -d sourcedb -s OGG_SRVC
```

6. Once the `OGG_SRVC` service has been created from the preceding code, you must add it to your `tnsnames.ora` file, for example, as follows:

```
OGG_SRVC =
(DESCRIPTION =
    (ADDRESS = (PROTOCOL = TCP)(HOST = hosta1-vip)(PORT = 1521))
    (ADDRESS = (PROTOCOL = TCP)(HOST = hosta2-vip)(PORT = 1521))
    (LOAD_BALANCE = NO)
    (CONNECT_DATA =
        (SERVER = DEDICATED)
        (SERVICE_NAME = OGG_SRVC)
    )
)
```

7. For very slow networks, or networks with bandwidth limitations, you would benefit highly by enabling network compression in the data pump extract. We can do it using the following example:

Example: enabling compression for your trail files in flight as follows:

```
rmthost london mgrport 7809 tcpbufsize 1000000 compress
```

How it works...

In larger implementation systems, where large volume of data is being replicated, there will likely be more parallel processes running in both the source and target sites to improve data throughput in your environment. Oracle GoldenGate can support up to 5,000 concurrent Extract and Replicat processes per instance. Each Extract and Replicat process needs a minimum of 20-55 MB of memory. Memory can grow per process depending on the size and mix of concurrent transactions.

Oracle GoldenGate memory consumption is only restrained by the physical memory managed by the operating system, and not the Oracle GoldenGate program. However, in recent releases, Oracle GoldenGate cache manager takes advantage of the operating system's memory management functions, thus making more efficient use of memory.

It is advisable to create a separate filesystem for your OGG installation software as follows:

 ▸ 50-150 MB, depending on your platform and database. This includes the compressed download distribution file and the uncompressed files.
 ▸ For each OGG installation, ensure you have at least 40 MB of free space for the working directories and binaries.

If you are installing on a cluster environment, such as Oracle RAC, ensure the software distribution is on a shared filesystem so that each instance of your RAC database can access the binaries.

An additional 1 GB of disk space is required to hold your OGG trail files. This is an estimate and your environment may need more or less, depending of the amount of data volume to process and also factoring in the retention period of these trail files. I've seen sites where trail files are kept for seven days before being purged, or for one to two days. Therefore, the retention period will add to your storage requirements.

Regarding ping stats: ping was issued with a count of 0.8 **Round Trip Time** (**RTT**) to gauge for any latency fluctuation in the network. The RTT 0.8 ms is then multiplied by the network bandwidth (for example, your interface card speed). We divide the result by 8 to determine the number of bytes (8 bits = 1 byte). This value yields 1,000,000 bytes. Therefore the data pump extract parameter should reflect the following: tcpbufsize 1000000, for your optimum transfer rate.

Use the compress option of the RMTHOST parameter to compress data before it is sent over the wire. You would normally consider this given that your enterprise may have a very busy network, or if your network is very slow due to low bandwidth throughput. Make sure you weigh in the benefits of compression against the CPU resources that are required to perform the compression.

Installing Oracle GoldenGate (Simple)

This recipe will go through the process of downloading and installing OGG on Unix.

Getting ready

You could obtain the OGG software either from `http://otn.oracle.com` (click on the **DOWNLOADS** tab, scroll down to the **Middleware** section, and click on **GoldenGate**) for trial purposes, or if you have a valid email / password account go to My Oracle Support and buy a license to use OGG, from `http://edelivery.oracle.com`.

In this example, both source and target environments are of identical configurations. Of course, in real-world examples, there will be mixed platform configurations as well. The configuration used in this example is as follows:

- ▸ Platform: AIX
- ▸ Operating System Version: 6.1
- ▸ Database Version: Oracle 11.2.0.3.0
- ▸ GoldenGate Version: 11.2.1.0.1

How to do it...

Steps for installing Oracle GoldenGate on the source host are as follows:

1. Log in to the source host as the "oracle" user.
2. Create an installation directory to host the OGG binaries. I'm using a sandbox; ideally, you'll have a specific mount point for OGG. We do it using the following command:

   ```
   $ mkdir -p /u01/app/oracle/gg
   ```

3. Change the directory to the top level directory of your software installation, as follows:

   ```
   $ cd /u01/app/oracle/gg
   ```

4. Download the OGG software to the download directory created in step 3.
5. When you download the OGG software, make sure you choose the correct software for your operating system and database version from either **Oracle Technology Network** (**OTN**) or Oracle eDelivery.

6. After downloading the ZIP file for AIX, we do the listing of directory contents by using the following command:

```
$ ls -l
```

The output of the preceding command will be as follows:

```
-rw-r--r--    1 oracle    oinstall    49963147 Nov 14 13:51
ogg112101_ggs_AIX_ppc_ora11g_64bit.zip
```

7. Now we're ready to inflate the ZIP file, we do it by using following command:

```
$ unzip ogg112101_ggs_AIX_ppc_ora11g_64bit.zip
```

The output of the preceding command will be as follows:

```
Archive:  ogg112101_ggs_AIX_ppc_ora11g_64bit.zip
  inflating: ggs_AIX_ppc_ora11g_64bit.tar
  inflating: OGG_WinUnix_Rel_Notes_11.2.1.0.1.pdf
  inflating: Oracle GoldenGate 11.2.1.0.1 README.doc
  inflating: Oracle GoldenGate 11.2.1.0.1 README.txt
```

8. The inflated files contain another tar file which contains the actual software distribution. We need to untar this file, using the following command:

```
$ tar xvf ggs_AIX_ppc_ora11g_64bit.tar
```

9. Complete untaring the file. You now have successfully installed the OGG distribution.

10. Next we need to ensure we set up our environment variables accordingly. In your current shell, you need to export the following variables:

```
$ export ORACLE_HOME=/u01/app/oracle/product/11.2.0/db_1
$ export ORACLE_SID=SRC100
```

11. We would now be setting the library path for AIX. For AIX systems, this export is mandatory and is done by using the following command:

```
$ export LIBPATH="${ORACLE_HOME}/lib
```

12. Next step is to invoke Oracle GoldenGate to create the `subdirs` directories where the parameter files, trail files, temp directory, traces, and so on will be stored. Change the directory to your OGG home and create the following subdirectories:

```
$ cd /u01/app/oracle/gg
$ ./ggsci
GGSCI> create subdirs
```

The output of the preceding commands will be as follows:

```
Creating subdirectories under current directory /u01/app/oracle/gg


Parameter files              /u01/app/oracle/gg/dirprm: already
exists
Report files                 /u01/app/oracle/gg/dirrpt: created
Checkpoint files             /u01/app/oracle/gg/dirchk: created
Process status files         /u01/app/oracle/gg/dirpcs: created
SQL script files             /u01/app/oracle/gg/dirsql: created
Database definitions files   /u01/app/oracle/gg/dirdef: created
Extract data files           /u01/app/oracle/gg/dirdat: created
Temporary files              /u01/app/oracle/gg/dirtmp: created
Stdout files                 /u01/app/oracle/gg/dirout: created
```

13. At this stage we have completed the OGG installation, we now exit the installation using the following command:

```
GGSCI> exit
```

The steps for installing Oracle GoldenGate in the target host are the same as the preceding steps. Repeat the steps from 1 to 13 in your target host.

How it works...

In order to download the correct Oracle GoldenGate version for your platform and database you must know your operating system version and chipset (x86, x86 64bit, IA64, and so on) including your database version and kernel bit information (32-bit or 64-bit).

After you have downloaded the software and installed it, you need to update your environment settings. Make sure you do this on the target host as well.

You need to ensure you have your `ORACLE_HOME` and `ORACLE_SID` variables set accordingly in your environment.

If you're using the Korn Shell/Bourne Shell then you can set these in your `.profile` file. If you're using the Bash shell, then you can update your `.bash_profile` file. For example, we perform the update using the following command:

```
$ vi .bash_profile
```

And add the following command lines to the file:

```
export ORACLE_HOME="/u01/app/oracle/product/11.2.0/db_1"
export ORACLE_SID="SRC100"
export LIBPATH="{ORACLE_HOME}/lib"
```

Then save the file and exit.

`LIBPATH` was used in our preceding recipe that is specific to AIX. For other platforms, the shared libraries are referenced in the following table:

Platform	Environment variable
HP-UX	`SHLIB_PATH`
Sun Solaris	`LD_LIBRARY_PATH`
HP True64 (OSF/1)	
Linux	

In 64-bit platforms with 32-bit Oracle databases, OGG requires the `LD_LIBRARY_PATH` variable to include the 32-bit Oracle libraries.

When Oracle GoldenGate and the database are running on the same server, the following software must have the same bit type; all either 32-bit, 64-bit, or IA64:

- Oracle library versions
- Oracle GoldenGate version
- Database versions

When Oracle GoldenGate connects remotely to the database server via SQL*Net, the following processes are required:

- Extract
- Replicat

The Oracle client library and the Oracle GoldenGate build of both Extract and Replicat processes must have the same Oracle version, bit type, and operating system version.

 The top level software directory on the target server in my sandbox is `/u01/app/oracle/goldengate`. Although this could be any arbitrary directory path, in real-world environments you would ideally create a standard mount point location for all your OGG installations across the enterprise.

Creating one-way replication (Simple)

Here we'll be utilizing the demo scripts included in the OGG software distribution to implement a basic homogenous (Oracle-to-Oracle) replication.

Getting ready

You need to ensure your Oracle database is in archivelog mode. If your database is not in archivelog mode, you won't be able to recover your database due to media corruption or user errors.

How to do it...

The steps for creating one-way replication are as follows:

1. Check whether supplemental logging is enabled on your source database using the following command:

    ```
    SQL> select supplemental_log_data_min from v$database;
    ```

    The output of the preceding command will be as follows:

    ```
    SUPPLEME

    ----------------

    NO
    ```

2. Enable supplemental logging using the following command:

    ```
    SQL> alter database add supplemental log data;
    SQL> select supplemental_log_data_min from v$database;
    ```

    The output of the preceding command will be as follows:

    ```
    SUPPLEME

    ----------------

    YES
    ```

3. Let's run the demo script to create a couple of tables in the scott schema. You need to know the scott schema password, which is tiger by default. We do it using following command:

    ```
    $ cd /u01/app/oracle/gg
    $ ./ggsci
    $ sqlpus scott
    Enter password:
    SQL> @demo_ora_create.sql
    ```

The output of the preceding command will be as follows:

```
DROP TABLE tcustmer
         *
ERROR at line 1:
ORA-00942: table or view does not exist
Table created.
DROP TABLE tcustord
        *
ERROR at line 1:
ORA-00942: table or view does not exist
Table created.
```

4. You must add the checkpoint table, do it as follows:

```
$ cd /u01/app/oracle/gg
$ vi GLOBALS
```

Add the following entry to the file:

```
CheckPointTable ogg.chkpt
```

Save the file and exit.

5. Next create the checkpoint table using the following command:

```
$ ./ggsci
GGSCI> add checkpointtable
GGSCI> info checkpointtable
```

The output of the preceding command will be as follows:

```
No checkpoint table specified, using GLOBALS specification (ogg.
chkpt)...
Checkpoint table ogg.chkpt created 2012-10-31 12:39:38.
```

6. Set up the MANAGER parameter file using the following command:

```
$ cd /u01/app/oracle/gg/dirprm
$ vi mgr.prm
```

Add the following lines to the file:

```
PORT 7809
DYNAMICPORTLIST 7810-7849
AUTORESTART er *, RETRIES 6, WAITMINUTES 1, RESETMINUTES 10
PURGEOLDEXTRACTS /u01/app/oracle/gg/dirdat/*, USECHECKPOINTS,
MINKEEPDAYS 2
```

Save the file and exit.

7. Start the manager using the following command:

```
$ cd /u01/app/oracle/gg
$ ggsci
GGSCI> start mgr
GGSCI> info mgr
```

The output of the preceding command will be as follows:

```
GGSCI> info all
Program      Status       Group     Lag at Chkpt   Time Since Chkpt
MANAGER      RUNNING
```

8. Create a TNS entry in the database home so that the extract can connect to the **Automatic Storage Management** (**ASM**) instance, using the following command:

```
$ cd $ORACLE_HOME/network/admin
$ vi tnsnames.ora
```

Add the following TNS entry:

```
ASMGG =
  (DESCRIPTION =
    (ADDRESS =
        (PROTOCOL = IPC)
        (key=EXTPROC1521)
    )
    (CONNECT_DATA=
      (SID=+ASM)
    )
  )
```

Save the file and exit.

9. Create a user `asmgg` with the sysdba role in the ASM instance. Connect to the ASM instance as `sys` user using the following command:

```
$ sqlplus sys/<password>@asmgg as sysasm
```

The output of the preceding command will be as follows:

```
SQL*Plus: Release 11.2.0.3.0 Production on Thu Nov 15 14:24:20
2012
Copyright (c) 1982, 2011, Oracle.  All rights reserved.
Connected to:
Oracle Database 11g Enterprise Edition Release 11.2.0.3.0 - 64bit
Production
With the Automatic Storage Management option
```

The user is created using the following command:

```
SQL> create user asmgg identified by asmgg ;
```

We will get the following output message:

```
User created.
```

Provide the sysdba role to the user ASMGG using the following command:

```
SQL> grant sysdba to asmgg ;
```

We will get the following output message:

```
Grant succeeded.
```

10. Let's add supplemental logging to the source tables using the following commands:

```
$ cd /u01/app/oracle/gg
$ ./ggsci
GGSCI> add trandata scott.tcustmer
```

The output will be as follows:

```
Logging of supplemental redo data enabled for table SCOTT.
TCUSTMER.
```

Then type the following command:

```
GGSCI> add trandata scott.tcustord
```

The output message will be as follows:

```
Logging of supplemental redo data enabled for table SCOTT.
TCUSTORD.
```

The next command to be executed is:

```
GGSCI> info trandata scott.tcustmer
```

The output message will be as follows:

```
Logging of supplemental redo log data is disabled for table OGG.
TCUSTMER.
```

The next command to be used is:

```
GGSCI> info trandata scott.tcustord
```

The output will be as follows:

```
Logging of supplemental redo log data is disabled for table OGG.
TCUSTORD.
```

11. Create the extract parameter file for data capture using the following command:

```
$ cd /u01/app/oracle/gg/dirprm
$ vi ex01sand.prm
```

Add the following lines to the file:

```
EXTRACT ex01sand

SETENV (ORACLE_SID="SRC100")
SETENV (ORACLE_HOME="/u01/app/oracle/product/11.2.0/db_1")
SETENV (NLS_LANG="AMERICAN_AMERICA.AL32UTF8")

USERID ogg, PASSWORD ogg

TRANLOGOPTIONS EXCLUDEUSER ogg
TRANLOGOPTIONS ASMUSER asmgg@ASMGG ASMPASSWORD asmgg

-- Trail File location locally

EXTTRAIL /u01/app/oracle/gg/dirdat/pr

DISCARDFILE /u01/app/oracle/gg/dirrpt/ex01sand.dsc, PURGE
DISCARDROLLOVER AT 01:00 ON SUNDAY

TABLE    SCOTT.TCUSTMER ;
TABLE    SCOTT.TCUSTORD ;
```

Save the file and exit.

12. Let's add the Extract process and start it. We do it by using the following command:

```
$ cd /u01/app/oracle/gg
$ ./ggsci
GGSCI> add extract ex01sand tranlog begin now
```

The output of the preceding command will be as follows:

```
EXTRACT added.
```

The following command adds the location of the trail files and size for each trail created:

```
GGSCI> add exttrail /u01/app/oracle/gg/dirdat/pr extract ex01sand
megabytes 2
```

The output of the preceding command will be as follows:

```
EXTTRAIL added.
GGSCI> start ex01sand
Sending START request to MANAGER ...
EXTRACT EX01SAND starting
GGSCI> info all
```

Program	Status	Group	Lag at Chkpt	Time Since Chkpt
MANAGER	RUNNING			
EXTRACT	RUNNING	EX01SAND	00:00:00	00:00:06

13. Next we'll create the data pump parameter file using the following command:

```
$ cd /u01/app/oracle/gg/dirprm
$ vi pp01sand.prm
```

Add the following lines to the file:

```
EXTRACT pp01sand

PASSTHRU

RMTHOST hostb MGRPORT 7820
RMTTRAIL /u01/app/oracle/goldengate/dirdat/rp

DISCARDFILE /u01/app/oracle/gg/dirrpt/pp01sand.dsc, PURGE

-- Tables for transport

TABLE   SCOTT.TCUSTMER ;
TABLE   SCOTT.TCUSTORD ;
```

Save the file and exit.

14. Add the data pump process and final configuration on the source side as follows:

```
GGSCI> add extract pp01sand exttrailsource /u01/app/oracle/gg/
dirdat/pr
```

The output of the preceding command will be as follows:

```
EXTRACT added.
```

The following command points the pump to drop the trail files to the remote location:

```
GGSCI> add rmttrail /u01/app/oracle/goldengate/dirdat/rp extract
pp01sand megabytes 2
```

The output of the preceding command will be as follows:

```
RMTTRAIL added.
```

15. Then we execute the following command:

```
GGSCI> info all
```

The output of the preceding command will be as follows:

Program	Status	Group	Lag at Chkpt	Time Since Chkpt
MANAGER	RUNNING			
EXTRACT	RUNNING	EXPR610	00:00:00	00:00:05
EXTRACT	STOPPED	PP01SAND	00:00:00	00:00:55

We're not going to start the data pump (pump) at this point since the manager does not yet exist at the target site.

Perform the following actions on the target server.

We've now completed most of our steps on the source system. We'll have to come back to the source server to start the pump a little later. Now, we'll move on to our target server where we'll have to set up the Replicat process in order to receive and apply the changes received from the source database. Perform the following actions on the target database:

1. Create tables on the target host using the following command:

```
$ cd /u01/app/oracle/goldengate
$ sqlplus scott/tiger
SQL> @demo_ora_create.sql
```

The output of the preceding command will be as follows:

```
DROP TABLE tcustmer
       *
ERROR at line 1:
ORA-00942: table or view does not exist
Table created.
DROP TABLE tcustord
       *
ERROR at line 1:
ORA-00942: table or view does not exist


Table created.
```

2. Let's add the checkpoint table as a global parameter using the following command:

    ```
    $ cd /u01/app/oracle/goldengate
    $ vi GLOBALS
    ```

    Add the following line to the file:

    ```
    CheckPointTable ogg.chkpt
    ```

    Save the file and exit.

3. Create the checkpoint table using the following command:

    ```
    $ cd ..
    $ ./ggsci
    GGSCI> dblogin userid ogg password ogg
    GGSCI> add checkpointtable
    ```

    Then execute the following command:

    ```
    $ cd /u01/app/oracle/goldengate/dirprm
    $ vi mgr.prm
    ```

    Add the following lines to the file:

    ```
    PORT 7820
    DYNAMICPORTLIST 7821-7849
    AUTORESTART er *, RETRIES 6, WAITMINUTES 1, RESETMINUTES 10
    PURGEOLDEXTRACTS /u01/app/oracle/goldengate/dirdat/*,
    USECHECKPOINTS, MINKEEPFILES 2
    ```

    Save the file and exit

4. Start the manager using the following command:

```
$ cd /u01/app/oracle/goldengate
$ ./ggsci
GGSCI> start mgr
GGSCI> info mgr

GGSCI> info all
```

We will get the following output:

```
Program      Status      Group      Lag at Chkpt  Time Since Chkpt
MANAGER      RUNNING
```

5. Edit the parameter file using the following command, now we're ready to create the replicat parameter file:

```
$ cd /u01/app/oracle/goldengate/dirprm
$ vi re01sand.prm
```

Add the following lines to the file:

```
REPLICAT re01sand

SETENV (ORACLE_SID="TRG101")
SETENV (ORACLE_HOME="/u01/app/oracle/product/11.1.0/db_1")
SETENV (NLS_LANG = "AMERICAN_AMERICA.AL32UTF8")

USERID ogg PASSWORD ogg

DISCARDFILE /u01/app/oracle/goldengate/dirrpt/re01sand.dsc, APPEND
DISCARDROLLOVER at 01:00

ReportCount Every 30 Minutes, Rate
REPORTROLLOVER at 01:30

DBOPTIONS DEFERREFCONST
ASSUMETARGETDEFS

MAP SCOTT.TCUSTMER , TARGET SCOTT.TCUSTMER ;
MAP SCOTT
```

Save the file and exit.

6. We now add and start the Replicat process using the following commands:

```
$ cd ..
```

The following extrail location must match exactly as in the pump's rmttrail location on the source server:

```
$ ./ggsci
GGSCI> add replicat re01sand exttrail /u01/app/oracle/goldengate/
dirdat/rp checkpointtable ogg.chkpt


GGSCI> start re01sand
```

The output of the preceding command will be as follows:

```
Sending START request to MANAGER ...
REPLICAT RE01SAND starting
```

Then we execute the following command:

```
GGSCI> info all
```

The output of the preceding command will be as follows:

Program	Status	Group	Lag at Chkpt	Time Since Chkpt
MANAGER	RUNNING			
REPLICAT	RUNNING	RE01SAND	00:00:00	00:00:01

7. Let's go back to the source host and start the pump using the following command:

```
$ cd /u01/app/oracle/gg
$ ./ggsci
GGSCI> start pp01sand
```

The output of the preceding command will be as follows:

```
Sending START request to MANAGER ...
EXTRACT PP01SAND starting
```

8. Next we use the demo insert script to add rows to source tables that should replicate to the target tables. We can do it using the following commands:

```
$ cd /u01/app/oracle/gg
$ sqlplus scott/tiger
SQL> @demo_ora_insert
```

The output of the preceding command will be as follows:

```
1 row created.
1 row created.
1 row created.
1 row created.
Commit complete.
```

9. To verify that the 4 rows just created have been captured at the source use the following commands:

```
$ ./ggsci
GGSC>stats ex01sand totalsonly scott.*
```

The output of the preceding command will be as follows:

```
Sending STATS request to EXTRACT EX01SAND ...


Start of Statistics at 2012-11-30 20:22:37.


Output to /u01/app/oracle/gg/dirdat/pr:
… truncated for brevity
*** Latest statistics since 2012-11-30 20:17:38 ***
        Total inserts                         4.00
        Total updates                         0.00
        Total deletes                         0.00
        Total discards                        0.00
        Total operations                      4.00
```

10. To verify if the pump has shipped to the target server use the following command:

```
GGSCI> stats pp01sand totalsonly scott.*
```

The output of the preceding command will be as follows:

```
Sending STATS request to EXTRACT PP01SAND ...
Start of Statistics at 2012-11-30 20:24:56.
Output to /u01/app/oracle/goldengate/dirdat/rp:
```

```
Cumulative totals for specified table(s):
… cut for brevity
*** Latest statistics since 2012-11-30 20:18:14 ***
        Total inserts                          4.00
        Total updates                          0.00
        Total deletes                          0.00
        Total discards                         0.00
        Total operations                       4.00
End of Statistics.
```

11. And finally if they have been applied at the target, the next command is performed at the target server as follows:

```
$ ./ggsci

GGSCI> stats re01sand totalsonly scott.*
```

The output of the preceding command will be as follows:

```
Sending STATS request to REPLICAT RE01SAND ...
Start of Statistics at 2012-11-30 20:28:01.
Cumulative totals for specified table(s):
...
*** Latest statistics since 2012-11-30 20:18:20 ***
        Total inserts                          4.00
        Total updates                          0.00
        Total deletes                          0.00
        Total discards                         0.00
        Total operations                       4.00
End of Statistics.
```

How it works...

Supplemental logging must be turned on at the database level and subsequently at the table level as well, for those tables you would like to replicate. For a one-way replication, this is done at the source table. There isn't a need to turn on supplemental logging at the target site, if the target site in turn is not a source to other targets or to itself.

A database user ogg is created in order to administer the OGG schema. This user is solely used for the purpose of administering OGG in the database.

Checkpoints are needed by both the source and target servers; these are structures that persist to disk as a known position in the trail file. You would start from these after an expected or unexpected shutdown of the OGG process.

The PORT parameter in the mgr.prm file specifies the port to which the MGR should bind and start listening for connection requests. If the manager is down, then connections can't be established and you'll receive TCP connection errors. The only necessary parameter required is the port number itself. Also, the PURGEOLDEXTRACT parameter is a nice way to keep your trail files to a minimum size so that they don't store indefinitely and finally run out of space in your filesystem. In this example, we're asking the manager to purge trail files and keep the files from the last two days on disk.

If your Oracle database is using an ASM instance, then OGG needs to establish a connection to the ASM instance in order to read the online-redo logs. You must ensure that you either use the sys schema or create a user (such as asmgg) with SYSDBA privileges for authentication.

Since we need a supplemental log at the table level, add trandata does precisely this.

Now we'll focus on some of the EXTRACT (ex01sand) data capture parameters. For one thing, you'll notice that we need to supply the extract with credentials to the database and the ASM instance in order to scan the online-redo logs for committed transactions. The following lines tell OGG to exclude the user ogg from capture. The second tranlogoptions is how the extract authenticates to the ASM instance.

```
USERID ogg, PASSWORD ogg

TRANLOGOPTIONS EXCLUDEUSER ogg
TRANLOGOPTIONS ASMUSER asmgg@ASMGG ASMPASSWORD asmgg
```

If you're using Oracle version 10gR2 and later versions of 10gR2, or Oracle 11.2.0.2 and later, you could use the newer ASM API tranlogoptions DBLOGREADER rather than the ASMUSER. The API uses the database connection rather than connecting to the ASM instance to read the online-redo logs.

The following two lines in the extract tell the extract where to place the trail files, with a prefix of pr followed by 6 digits that increment once each file rolls over to the next file generation. The DISCARDFILE by convention has the same name as the extract but with an extension .dsc for discard. If, for any reason, OGG can't capture a transaction, it will throw the text and SQL to this file for later investigation.

```
EXTTRAIL /u01/app/oracle/gg/dirdat/pr

DISCARDFILE /u01/app/oracle/gg/dirrpt/ex01sand.dsc, PURGE
```

Tables or schemas are captured with the following syntax in the extract file:

```
TABLE    SCOTT.TCUSTMER ;
TABLE    SCOTT.TCUSTORD ;
```

The specification can vary and use wildcards as well. Say you want to capture the entire schema, you could specify this as `TABLE SCOTT.* ;`.

In the following code the first command adds the extract with the option `tranlog begin now` telling OGG to start capturing changes using the online-redo logs as of now. The second command tells the extract where to store the trail files with a size not exceeding 2 MB.

```
GGSCI> add extract ex01sand tranlog begin now
GGSCI> add exttrail /u01/app/oracle/gg/dirdat/pr extract ex01sand
megabytes 2
```

Now, the `PUMP` (data pump; `pp01sand`) is an optional, but highly recommended extract whose sole purpose is to perform all of the TCP/IP activity; for example, transporting the trail files to the target site. This is beneficial because we alleviate the capture process from performing any of the TCP/IP activity.

The parameters in the following snippet tell the pump to send the data as is with the `PASSTHRU` parameter. This is the optimal and preferred method if there isn't any data transformation along the way. The `RMTHOST` parameter specifies the destination host and the port to which the remote manager is listening, for example, port 7820. If the manager port is not running at the target, the destination host will refuse the connection; that is why we did not start the pump early on during our work on the source host.

```
PASSTHRU

RMTHOST hostb MGRPORT 7820
RMTTRAIL /u01/app/oracle/goldengate/dirdat/rp
```

The `RMTTRAIL` specifies where the trail file will be stored at the remote host with a prefix of `rp` followed by a 6 digit number sequentially increasing as the files roll over after a specified size has reached.

Finally, at the destination host, `hostb`, the Replicat process (`re01sand`) is the applier where the SQL is replayed in the target database. The following two lines in the parameter file specify how the Replicat knows to map source and target data as it comes in by way of the trail files:

```
MAP SCOTT.TCUSTMER , TARGET SCOTT.TCUSTMER ;
MAP SCOTT.TCUSTORD , TARGET SCOTT.TCUSTORD ;
```

The target tables don't necessarily have to be of the same schema names as in the preceding example, but they could have been applied to a different schema altogether if that was the requirement.

Creating bidirectional replication (Simple)

We'll pick up from the previous recipe and configure the target host to also capture and deliver changes to the same set of tables on the source host.

Getting ready

Repeat steps 1 to 14 followed by steps 1 to 7 from the recipe *Creating One-Way Replication (Simple)*. The rest of the steps prepare the target host to capture changes and deliver them to the applier on the source host.

How to do it...

The steps for bidirectional replication are as follows:

1. Enable supplemental logging on the target database in order to capture appropriate database changes.

    In our previous recipe, we didn't have to enable supplemental logging on the target because it was not subject to propagating changes. However, in a two-way replication, we propagate in both the ways, as follows:

    ```
    SQL> select supplemental_log_data_min from v$database;
    ```

    We will get the following output:

    ```
    SUPPLEME

    -----------------

    NO
    ```

    The next set of commands to be executed is as follows:

    ```
    SQL> alter database add supplemental log data;
    SQL> select supplemental_log_data_min from v$database;
    ```

    We will get the following output:

    ```
    SUPPLEME

    -----------------

    YES
    ```

2. Create a TNS entry in the database home so that the extract can connect to the ASM instance using the following command:

    ```
    $ cd $ORACLE_HOME/network/admin
    $ vi tnsnames.ora
    ```

Add the following TNS entry:

```
ASMGG =
  (DESCRIPTION =
    (ADDRESS =
      (PROTOCOL = IPC)
      (key=EXTPROC1521)
    )
    (CONNECT_DATA=
      (SID=+ASM)
    )
  )
```

Save the file and exit.

3. Create a user `asmgg` with the sysdba role in the ASM instance using the following command:

```
$ sqlplus sys/<password>@asmgg as sysasm
```

The output for the preceding command will be as follows:

```
SQL*Plus: Release 11.2.0.3.0 Production on Thu Nov 15 14:24:20
2012

Copyright (c) 1982, 2011, Oracle.  All rights reserved.

Connected to:

Oracle Database 11g Enterprise Edition Release 11.2.0.3.0 - 64bit
Production

With the Automatic Storage Management option
```

Then we execute the following two commands:

```
SQL> create user asmgg identified by asmgg ;
```

The output for the preceding command will be as follows:

```
User created.
```

and

```
SQL> grant sysdba to asmgg ;
```

The output for the preceding command will be as follows:

```
Grant succeeded.
```

4. Let's add supplemental logging to the tables using the following commands:

```
$ cd /u01/app/oracle/goldengate
$ ./ggsci
GGSCI> add trandata scott.tcustmer
```

The output for the preceding commands will be as follows :

```
Logging of supplemental redo data enabled for table SCOTT.
TCUSTMER.
```

```
GGSCI> add trandata scott.tcustord
```

The output for the preceding command is as follows:

```
Logging of supplemental redo data enabled for table SCOTT.
TCUSTORD.
```

```
GGSCI> info trandata scott.tcustmer
```

The output for the preceding command is as follows:

```
Logging of supplemental redo log data is disabled for table OGG.
TCUSTMER.
```

```
GGSCI> info trandata scott.tcustord
```

5. Create the extract parameter file for data capture using the following command:

   ```
   $ cd /u01/app/oracle/goldengate/dirprm
   ```

   ```
   $ vi ex01sand.prm
   ```

   Add the following lines to the file:

   ```
   EXTRACT ex01sand

   SETENV (ORACLE_SID="TGT101")
   SETENV (ORACLE_HOME="/u01/app/oracle/product/11.2.0/db_1")
   SETENV (NLS_LANG="AMERICAN_AMERICA.AL32UTF8")

   USERID ogg, PASSWORD ogg

   TRANLOGOPTIONS EXCLUDEUSER ogg
   TRANLOGOPTIONS ASMUSER asmgg@ASMGG ASMPASSWORD asmgg

   -- Trail File location locally

   EXTTRAIL /u01/app/oracle/goldengate/dirdat/pr

   DISCARDFILE /u01/app/oracle/goldengate/dirrpt/ex01sand.dsc, PURGE
   DISCARDROLLOVER AT 01:00 ON SUNDAY

   TABLE   SCOTT.TCUSTMER ;
   TABLE   SCOTT.TCUSTORD ;
   ```

   Save the file and exit.

6. Let's add the Extract process and start it by using the following commands:

```
$ cd /u01/app/oracle/goldengate
$ ./ggsci
GGSCI> add extract ex01sand tranlog begin now
```

The output for the preceding command is as follows:

```
EXTRACT added.
```

```
GGSCI> add exttrail /u01/app/oracle/goldengate/dirdat/pr extract
ex01sand megabytes 2
```

The output for the preceding command is as follows:

```
EXTTRAIL added.
```

```
GGSCI> start ex01sand
```

The output for the preceding command is as follows:

```
Sending START request to MANAGER ...
EXTRACT EX01SAND starting
```

```
GGSCI> info all
```

The output for the preceding command is as follows:

Program	Status	Group	Lag at Chkpt	Time Since Chkpt
MANAGER	RUNNING			
MANAGER	RUNNING			
EXTRACT	RUNNING	EX01SAND	00:00:00	00:00:06
REPLICAT	RUNNING	RE01SAND	00:00:00	00:00:07

7. Next we'll create the data pump parameter file using the following commands:

```
$ cd /u01/app/oracle/goldengate/dirprm
$ vi pp01sand.prm
```

Add the following lines to the file:

```
EXTRACT pp01sand

PASSTHRU
```

```
RMTHOST hosta MGRPORT 7809
RMTTRAIL /u01/app/oracle/gg/dirdat/pa

DISCARDFILE /u01/app/oracle/goldengate/dirrpt/pp01sand.dsc, PURGE

-- Tables for transport

TABLE    SCOTT.TCUSTMER ;
TABLE    SCOTT.TCUSTORD ;
```

Save the file and exit.

8. Add the data pump process and final configuration on the target host using the following commands:

```
GGSCI> add extract pp01sand exttrailsource /u01/app/oracle/
goldengate/dirdat/pr
```

The output for the preceding command is as follows:

```
EXTRACT added.
```

```
GGSCI> add rmttrail /u01/app/oracle/gg/dirdat/pa extract pp01sand
megabytes 2
```

The output for the preceding command is as follows:

```
RMTTRAIL added.
```

```
GGSCI> start pp01sand
```

The output for the preceding command is as follows:

```
Sending START request to MANAGER ...
EXTRACT PP01SAND starting
```

```
GGSCI> info all
```

The output for the preceding command is as follows:

Program	Status	Group	Lag at Chkpt	Time Since Chkpt
MANAGER	RUNNING			
MANAGER	RUNNING			
EXTRACT	RUNNING	EX01SAND	00:00:00	00:00:06
EXTRACT	RUNNING	PP01SAND	00:00:00	00:00:02
REPLICAT	RUNNING	RE01SAND	00:00:00	00:00:07

9. Next, we'll move on to the source server and create the `REPLICAT` parameter file:

    ```
    $ cd /u01/app/oracle/gg/dirprm
    $ vi re01sand.prm
    ```

    Add the following lines to the file:

    ```
    REPLICAT re01sand

    SETENV (ORACLE_SID="SRC100")
    SETENV (ORACLE_HOME="/u01/app/oracle/product/11.1.0/db_1")
    SETENV (NLS_LANG = "AMERICAN_AMERICA.AL32UTF8")

    USERID ogg PASSWORD ogg

    DISCARDFILE /u01/app/oracle/gg/dirrpt/re01sand.dsc, APPEND
    DISCARDROLLOVER at 01:00

    ReportCount Every 30 Minutes, Rate
    REPORTROLLOVER at 01:30

    DBOPTIONS SUPPRESSTRIGGERS DEFERREFCONST
    ASSUMETARGETDEFS

    MAP SCOTT.TCUSTMER , TARGET SCOTT.TCUSTMER ;
    MAP SCOTT.TCUSTORD,  TARGET SCOTT.TCUSTORD ;
    ```

    Save the file and exit.

10. Now we're ready to complete our two-way replication by adding the Replicat process to apply the incoming changes.

    Add and start the Replicat using the following commands:

    ```
    $ cd ..
    $ ./ggsci
    GGSCI> add replicat re01sand exttrail /u01/app/oracle/gg/dirdat/pa
    checkpointtable ogg.chkpt

    GGSCI> start re01sand
    ```

    The output for the preceding command is as follows:

    ```
    Sending START request to MANAGER ...
    REPLICAT RE01SAND starting

    GGSCI> info all
    ```

The output for the preceding command is as follows:

Program	Status	Group	Lag at Chkpt	Time Since Chkpt
MANAGER	RUNNING			
EXTRACT	RUNNING	EX01SAND	00:00:00	00:00:07
EXTRACT	RUNNING	PP01SAND	00:00:00	00:00:03
REPLICAT	RUNNING	RE01SAND	00:00:00	00:00:06

11. Next let's validate that an insert will propagate from `hostb` to `hosta`.

    Perform the following actions on `hostb`:

    ```
    SQL> insert into scott.tcustmer values ('Tony','Ontario
    Inc','Toronto','ON') ;

    SQL> commit ;

    SQL> select * from scott.tcustmer;
    ```

    The output for the preceding command is as follows:

CUST	NAME	CITY	ST
WILL	BG SOFTWARE CO.	SEATTLE	WA
JANE	ROCKY FLYER INC.	DENVER	CO
Tony	Ontario Inc	Toronto	ON

12. Moving on to `hosta` we should execute the following commands to ensure our changes have been received and applied to the database:

    ```
    SQL> select * from scott.tcustmer ;
    ```

    The output for the preceding command is as follows:

CUST	NAME	CITY	ST
WILL	BG SOFTWARE CO.	SEATTLE	WA
JANE	ROCKY FLYER INC.	DENVER	CO
Tony	Ontario Inc	Toronto	ON

    Hence, we conclude that the insert was received and applied.

How it works...

Once again, we needed to add supplemental logging at the target host to both tables `scott.tcustmer` and `scott.tcustord` in order to add additional data in the redo stream. This was not necessary when these tables were subject to delivery only.

At `hostb` we already had a manager and Replicat process. We needed to configure an extract for data capture, to start scanning the online-redo logs and write out committed transactions to the trail files. We've kept the same two-letter prefix `pr` as we did on `hosta`. Remember that the letters can be any two arbitrary letters. The name of the data capture extract is also the same as in `hosta`. I did this just for simplicity sake. It does not have to be the same prefix. You ought to come up with a naming standard in your own organization for naming extracts and/or replicats.

Now that we've started capturing data, we need a pump to ship it to `hosta`. Again, I've chosen the same pump name for illustration purposes. Here we need to be a little more careful in choosing the remote trail name prefix as follows:

add rmttrail /u01/app/oracle/gg/dirdat/pa extract pp01sand megabytes 2

I've chosen the prefix "pa". You must ensure that you don't clobber any files on the remote host with an already used prefix as this may corrupt the trail files on the remote host. Point being, make sure you always choose unique prefixes for pumps, specifically if multiple pumps are shipping trail files to the same directory location.

Finally, back on `hosta`, the only process missing is the replicat which completes the multi-master implementation.

In this illustration of multi-master implementation, you need to consider the possibility of collisions, such as the same record being inserted or deleted simultaneously at both sites as it may violate constraints. In a real-world example, you may use a sequence to generate the Primary Key on the source and a differing sequence on the target so that collisions are minimized. Another alternative would be to use range partition on a numeric data type value based on different ranges between the source and target to avoid collision. And finally, if you know that the application code has the ability to ensure that a business rule between the source and target would never collide, then the implementation is trivial as the application will decide and manage the conflicts. Another important design factor is to use the Primary Key or Unique Key constraints for all objects being replicated; otherwise OGG will use all table columns to determine the uniqueness.

Creating heterogeneous replication (Simple)

In this section you'll experience the strength and flexibility of OGG to replicate disparate systems. In this recipe, we'll be using SQL Server 2008 as the source database and Oracle 11gR2 as the target database.

Getting ready

Once again, you can obtain the OGG software for SQL Server from `http://otn.oracle.com` (click on the **DOWNLOADS** tab, scroll down to the **Middleware** section, and click on **GoldenGate**) for trial purposes; alternatively, if you have a valid email / password account go to My Oracle Support and buy a license to use OGG, from `http://edelivery.oracle.com`.

How to do it...

One thing we need to cover quickly is the steps to install OGG for SQL Server, which are as follows:

1. Download and extract the OGG for SQL Server to a location of your choice, for example, `C:\GG`.

2. Open the command prompt and launch `ggsci` by running the following commands:

   ```
   C:\ggsci.exe
   GGSCI> create subdirs
   ```

3. Next we want to add the manager process as a Windows service; otherwise the manager process will stop upon session exit. Add it by using the following command:

   ```
   GGSCI>install addservice
   ```

   The output of the preceding command will be as follows :

   ```
   Service 'GGSMGR' created.
   ```

4. Edit the `Manager` parameter file as follows:

   ```
   GGSCI> edit param mgr
   ```

5. Add the following entries to the file:

   ```
   PORT 7809
   ```

   Save the file and exit.

6. Next start the manager by using the following command:

   ```
   GGSCI> start manager
   ```

Next we'll be creating an **Open DataBase Connectivity** (**ODBC**) connection on the source (SQL Server) database by using the following steps:

1. Create an ODBC connection for the data source name for userid ogg and password ogg

   Creating an ODBC connection is beyond the scope of this recipe. However, use the Windows ODBC wizard to guide you through with similar settings as follows:

   ```
   Data Source Name: sample
   Data Source Description: Sample_schema
   Server: servername\instance
   Database: sample
   Language: (Default)
   Translate Character Data: Yes
   Log Long Running Queries: No
   Log Driver Statistics: No
   Use Regional Settings: No
   Prepared Statements Option: Drop temporary procedures on
   disconnect
   Use Failover Server: No
   Use ANSI Quoted Identifiers: Yes
   Use ANSI Null, Paddings and Warnings: Yes
   Data Encryption: No
   ```

2. Add supplemental logging to the capture table changes on tcustmer as follows:

   ```
   C:\GG>ggsci.exe
   GGSCI> dblogin sourcedb sample
   GGSCI> add trandata dbo.tcustmer
   ```

3. Create a definitions file as follows:

   ```
   C:> cd C:\GG\dirprm
   C:\GG> notepad tcustmer.prm
   ```

   Add the following lines to the file:

   ```
   defsfile c:\GG\dirdef\tcustmer.def
   sourcedb sample
   table dbo.tcustmer
   ```

   Save the file and exit.

4. Generate the definitions file as follows:

   ```
   C:\GG\defgen paramfile c:\GG\dirprm\tcustmer.prm
   ```

5. Transfer the generated file `c:\GG\dirprm\tcustmer.def` to the target server under the OGG installation `/u01/app/oracle/gg/dirprm`. Use either the FTP or SFTP protocol to transfer the file.

6. For setting up the initial data load from SQL Server (source) use the following command:

```
GGSCI> edit param initload
```

Add the following lines to the file:

```
SOURCEISTABLE
SOURCEDB sample, USERID "ogg", PASSWORD "ogg"
RMTHOST unix_server_name, MGRPORT 7809
RMTFILE /u01/app/oracle/gg/dirdat/xp
TABLE dbo.tcustmer;
```

Save the file and exit.

We will now do the target setup (Oracle database server) as follows:

1. As we saw in the recipes *Installing Oracle GoldenGate (Simple)* and *Creating one-way replication (Simple)*, create a `Manager` parameter file and ensure you use port 7809 and start it. We only need the port number in the `mgr.prm` file for this task.

2. Create a one-time replicat parameter file called `tcust_ld` and start the replicat using the following commands:

```
$ cd /u01/app/oracle/gg/dirprm
$ vi tcust_ld.prm
```

Add the following lines to the file:

```
SPECIALRUN
ENDRUN
SETENV (ORACLE_SID="TRG101")
SETENV (ORACLE_HOME="/u01/app/oracle/product/11.2.0/db_1")
SETENV (NLS_LANG = "AMERICAN_AMERICA.AL32UTF8")

USERID ogg PASSWORD ogg
EXTFILE /u01/app/oracle/gg/dirdat/xp  # must match the rmtfile
from the # source  parameter file.
SOURCEDEFS /u01/app/oracle/gg/dirdef/tcustmer.def
MAP dbo."TCUSTMER" , TARGET SCOTT.TCUSTMER ;
```

The procedure for running the initial load from SQL Server is as follows:

1. Initiate the load from the SQL Server database by using the following command:

```
C:\GG\extract paramfile dirprm\initload.prm reportfile dirrpt\
initload.rpt
```

   Initiate the replication on the target server by using the following commands:

```
$ cd /u01/app/oracle/gg
$ ./replicat paramfile dirprm/tcust_ld.prm
```

How it works...

This entire setup is a one-time special run to get the initial table data from the source to the target; in other words, this is one method to instantiate to the target when a source database table has existing data. Once the table data has been completely copied, you will need to perform the same setup we've completed in *Installing Oracle GoldenGate (Simple)*.

The assumption here is that you already have a SQL server database in place. The first part during the preparation of the SQL server setup is to create a data source name via the ODBC connection for SQL Server authentication.

During the preparation on the source, you might have wondered about the source definition file in step 4. This file is absolutely necessary especially for data type mapping between different RDBMS types. It can also be used within the same RDBMS types if there are column mappings, transformation, data type size differences, database character set differences, and so on.

Steps 4 to 6 demonstrate how to create and generate the `tcustmer` table definition. The `defgen` utility takes as input the contents of `tcustmer.prm`. The result of running `defgen`, is a metadata file called `tcustmer.def` which you need to transfer to the target server and add it to either the replicat parameter file or the one-time special run parameter file so that OGG can perform appropriate data mapping on the target database. An example is as follows:

```
SOURCEISTABLE
SOURCEDB sample, USERID "ogg", PASSWORD "ogg"
```

`SOURCEISTABLE`, states that the source is the actual SQL Server table rather than the trail files. And finally the connection string to a SQL Server database uses the additional keyword `SOURCEDB` to identify the data source name.

On the target setup (Oracle database server), in the parameter file `tcust_ld.prm` we see a few new keywords we have not yet seen for an initial load:

- SPECIALRUN
- ENDRUN

`SPECIALRUN` implements an initial-load replicat as a one-time run that does not use checkpoints. `ENDRUN` directs the initial-load replicat to terminate when the load is finished.

`EXTFILE` in the Replicat process specifies the receiving files from the `RMTFILE` file in the Extract parameter file at the source. Finally, `SOURCEDEFS` must reference the `tcusmer.def` file which is the file you transferred from the source site to the target server. This is the definitions file that Oracle has to use in order to correctly interpret the SQL Server data types. In contrast, if you recall, in the recipe, *Implementing design considerations (Simple)* and the recipe, *Installing Oracle GoldenGate (Simple)* we used `ASSUMETARGETDEFS` because both source and target table definitions had identical data types, same **National Language Support** (**NLS**) language and character set.

Running the initial load and initiating the replication is a different method of invoking the OGG executables `extract` and `replicat` from the command line rather than within the OGG command line interface.

Configuring Oracle GoldenGate for High Availability (HA) (Simple)

Configuring and installing OGG for **High Availability** (**HA**) differs very little from a single instance on Unix/Linux. The main difference is in the filesystem set up in a cluster environment so that all nodes in the cluster have access to the OGG installation. Following are the main guidelines for Unix/Linux and Windows. The software can be downloaded either from OTN or Oracle's eDelivery site.

How to do it...

The steps for configuring Oracle GoldenGate for high availability are as follows:

1. The following simple steps will unpack the software distribution and create the appropriate directory structure for OGG on Unix/Linux systems. Extract the OGG `mediapack.zip` file to the system and directory where you want the OGG installation to reside, for example, `/GG mount point.`as shown in the following commands:

```
$ cd /GG
$ unzip mediapack.zip
$ ./GGSCI
GGSCI> create subdirs
GGSCI> exit
```

2. Next, if you are installing the software on a Windows server, follow these steps:

    1. Log on to one of the nodes on the cluster.
    2. Choose a drive for the installation. The drive must be a part of the resource group that contains the database, for example: `c:\GG`.

3. Unzip the downloaded file in your installation directory by using WinZip or a similar compression tool by using the following commands:

```
c:\GG\ggsci
GGSCI> create subdirs
GGSCI> exit
```

4. Copy the `category.dll` and `ggsmsg.dll` files from the OGG `root` directory to the `SYSTEM32` directory.

5. Specify a custom manager name as follows:

```
C:\GG
C:\GG\ggsci
GGSCI> edit param   ./GLOBALS
```

6. Add the following line to the file:

```
MGRSERVNAME   <NAME>
```

Where `<NAME>` is an arbitrary one-word name for the Manager service.

Save the file and exit.

We install the Manager as a Windows service so that it restarts upon server reboots.

7. Log in as the system administrator. Open the **Run** dialog then type cmd in the Run dialog box.

8. Change directory to the OGG installation home directory and install the service as follows:

```
C:\GG\install addservice autostart
```

How it works...

As a best practice it is better to install the OGG binaries entirely on shared storage. In this fashion, you can start the OGG processes from any node of the cluster and not worry about making any parameter changes.

For example if `/GG` is the chosen mount point to host your OGG installation, make sure that this mount point is mounted as a cluster filesystem by your system administrator in every host of the cluster.

If the node that started the manager and **Extract/Replicat** (**E/R**) processes fails, you can restart the manager and E/R processes from any of the surviving nodes as the checkpoint's integrity is maintained and you don't need to make any parameter file changes.

If you decide to install the OGG binaries locally on each node of the cluster, than you need to consider the following:

▸ Ensure you have the same location path of the OGG installation on each node.

▸ The following directories should be at a minimum located on the shared storage such as NetApp/DBFS storage to meet recovery requirements. You should create symbolic links from the installation directories to the shared storage mount point.

  ❑ br

  ❑ dirchk

  ❑ dirdat

  ❑ dirtmp

▸ Create a symbolic link, for example, from the installation directory to the shared directory, as follows:

```
$ ln -s /ggtrail/dirdat    /GG/dirdat
$ ln -s /ggtrail/dirchk    /GG/dirchk
$ ln -s /ggtrail/br        /GG/br
$ ln -s /ggtrail/dirtmp    /GG/dirtmp
```

The example uses `/ggtrail` as the shared location for the preceding directories.

▸ Another important point is to ensure your parameter files are identical on each node with the exception of the environment variables that access your Oracle RAC instance.

▸ Register the OGG Manager, and only the manager, as a cluster-managed resource. The OGG Manager process is the only cluster-management software that starts and stops since the Manager process is the parent process that manages all the other processes.

▸ Ensure that all nodes in which OGG software runs are selected as possible owners of the resource.

▸ Ensure that the Windows service Manager has the following dependencies from the Services control panel:

  ❑ The database resource

  ❑ The disk resource that contains the OGG installation

  ❑ The disk resource that contains the database transaction logs

  ❑ The disk resource that contains the database transaction log backup files

▸ If the cluster uses **Virtual IP** (**VIP**) such as Oracle ClusterWare, make sure the VIP is a static IP and available on the public subnet.

Configuring advanced settings (Simple)

In this section, we'll go over some advanced settings you could apply such as filtering, mapping, and data transformation.

How to do it...

OGG, in addition to replicating, allows data filtering, mapping, extraction, and transformation. Following, you'll discover a number of other functions that OGG can perform at either the source host or target host.

1. To capture all table changes in a schema, use the following wildcard specification:

   ```
   TABLE    SCOTT.* ;
   ```

2. When you need to exclude tables from being replicated, use the `tableexclude` clause as follows:

   ```
   TABLEEXLCUDE SCOTT.EMP ;
   TABLE    SCOTT.* ;
   ```

3. OGG allows you to filter data based on **Data Manipulation Language** (**DML**) as follows:

   ```
   ...
   IGNOREDELETES
   MAP SCOTT.* , TARGET SCOTT.* ;
   ...


   ...
   IGNOREUPDATES
   MAP SCOTT.* , TARGET SCOTT.* ;
   ...


   ...
   IGNOREINSERTS
   MAP SCOTT.* , TARGET SCOTT.* ;
   ...
   ```

4. You don't need to replicate every column of a table if the downstream system only requires a subset. We do it using the following:

   ```
   TABLE SCOTT.TCUSTMER, COLS(name,city,state) ;

   TABLE SCOTT.TCUSTMER, COLEXCEP(CODE_ID) ;
   ```

5. You can also ignore specific users from being captured. This is useful when the majority of schemas are being replicated with a few exceptions. An example is as follows:

```
...
TRANLOGOPTIONS EXCLUDEUSER <user>
...
```

6. Filter rows based on specific column values or when specific conditions are met. This can be done using the following format:

```
...
MAP SCOTT.TCUSTMER , TARGET SCOTT.TCUSTMER, WHERE (STATE in "CA")
;
...
```

7. Test for existence of a column in a data record as follows:

```
...
MAP SCOTT.EMP , TARGET SCOTT.EMP,WHERE (SAL=@PRESENT AND SALARY >
999)  ;
...
```

8. Data transformation is one of the tool's powerful capabilities for processes such as **ETL (Extract-Transformation-Load)**. It can be done for the following:

For mapping columns as follows:

```
...
MAP SCOTT.EMP , TARGET SCOTT.EMP, COLMAP(USEDEFAULTS, SAL=SALARY);
...
```

For entering default dates as follows:

```
...
MAP SCOTT.TCUSTORD , TARGET SCOTT.TCUSTORD, COLMAP(USEDEFAULTS,
ORDER_DATE=@DATENOW());
...
```

For concatenating strings as follows:

```
...
MAP SCOTT.EMP , TARGET SCOTT.EMP, COLMAP(USEDEFAULTS, NAME=@
STRCAT(FIRST_NAME," ",LAST_NAME));
...
```

9. We can perform the DML conversion in the following way. Inserts will become updates, updates will become deletes, and so on:

```
INSERTUPDATES
```

```
INSERTDELETES
```

```
UPDATEDELETES
```

10. For troubleshooting and reporting examples with OGG, tail the last 50 or so lines of the following file to view informational entries, warnings, and errors in OGG processing:

```
$ <OGG_HOME>/ggserr.log
```

11. Viewing information about an Extract/Replicat's checkpoints, RBA, and trailfile sequence can be done using the following commands:

```
$ GGSCI> info all | <group>
```

12. View the process report should the extract not start. Group can be an extract, data pump, or replicat.

```
$ GGSCI> view report <group>
GGSCI> start ex01sand
GGSCI> info all
```

The output would be as follows:

Program	Status	Group	Lag at Chkpt	Time Since Chkpt
MANAGER	RUNNING			
EXTRACT	STOPPED	EX01SAND	00:00:00	00:02:59
EXTRACT	RUNNING	PP01SAND	00:00:00	00:00:01
REPLICAT	RUNNING	RE01SAND	00:00:00	00:00:03

We can see that ex01sand won't start.

```
GGSCI> view report ex01sand
```

The output would be as follows:

```
2012-12-12 19:46:23   ERROR   OGG-00664  OCI Error beginning
session (status = 1017-ORA-01017: invalid username/password;
 logon denied).
```

```
2012-12-12 19:46:23   ERROR   OGG-01668  PROCESS ABENDING.
```

13. Edit the extract parameter file and make sure you update it with the correct password and then re-start the extract.

```
GGSCI> edit param ex01sand
```

Ensure you add the correct password.

```
GGSCI> start ex01sand
GGSCI> info all
```

The output should be as follows:

Program	Status	Group	Lag at Chkpt	Time Since Chkpt
MANAGER	RUNNING			
EXTRACT	RUNNING	EX01SAND	00:07:11	00:00:01
EXTRACT	RUNNING	PP01SAND	00:00:00	00:00:02
REPLICAT	RUNNING	RE01SAND	00:00:00	00:00:05

How it works...

Oracle GoldenGate is very flexible when it comes to dealing with data transformation and row filtering. Not only can it filter rows, but it can also filter based on the type of DML operations, such as updates, inserts, and deletes.

We've seen data capture by specifying explicitly the table name. However, you can use wild cards as well for an entire schema, or a specific table pattern such as TABLE SCOTT.*_TMP.

When you want to capture an entire schema and would like to exclude one or more tables from the capture process, make certain that the TABLEEXCLUDE clause is placed before the TABLE capture.

You might wonder why you would filter based on the DML statements, but consider the following; say you have source data where you have deletes but you don't want to propagate them to the target so as to keep a record of the row. You would ignore that delete operation on the target by stating IGNOREDELETES in the Replicat parameter file.

When extracting tables, you don't necessarily have to extract every column if they are not needed in the downstream system. You can use the COLS and COLSEXCEPT clause to control the columns of interest at the source.

Filtering rows is a nice way to ensure you only extract those rows with specific column values for delivery to your downstream system. Another useful operation is the presence or absence of particular column values such as the built in column function @PRESENT. GoldenGate has a number of functions that are preceded by the @ sign. Other examples are; @ABSENT and @NULL. Another way to filter is based on the FILTER clause on specific DML operations. We have not seen it yet, but here is an example:

```
TABLE SCOTT.SAL, FILTER (ON UPDATE, ON DELETE, SALARY > 499);
TABLE SCOTT.SAL, FILTER (ON INSERT, SALARY < 500);
```

When transforming data using COLMAP, you need to determine whether or not to use a definitions file. This depends whether or not source and target column structures are identical as defined by Oracle GoldenGate. GoldenGate considers columns identical when they have the same names, lengths, data type, semantics, and column order. As in the preceding example with data transformation, the @DATE function is synonymous to the SYSDATE function in Oracle and @STRCAT, is a string concatenation function.

The USEDEFAULTS clause applies default mapping rules to map source and target columns automatically if they have the same name.

DML conversions are interesting for the following reasons:

▶ The INSERTUPDATES clause converts source updates to inserts at the target. This is useful for maintaining a transaction history on that table.

▶ The INSERTDELETES clause converts source deletes to inserts at the target. This is necessary for retaining a history of all records that were present at the source.

▶ The UPDATEDELETES clause converts source deletes to updates at the target.

The error log file ggserr.log located at the root directory of your OGG installation, is one of the first sources of troubleshooting and diagnosing problems. It is a chronological log of events, commands, statistics, information, warnings, errors, and so on.

The INFO command is a quick way to view status information regarding the OGG processes, whether they are running, stopped, or abended, and, followed by the VIEW REPORT <group> as in the preceding example, will often point you to the root cause of the error.

Performing encryption in OGG (Simple)

In this section we'll discuss some OGG security features to secure our OGG environment and the data as it is being processed at rest and in flight. We'll briefly discuss **Transparent Data Encryption** (**TDE**) integration with OGG. Configuring and managing TDE and/or patching Oracle databases are beyond the scope of this book.

How to do it...

Data security and/or network security is an important design factor in today's world to prevent theft identity or any type of enterprise breaches to your organization. The steps to be performed are as follows:

1. Encrypt the OGG database user using the following command:

   ```
   $ ./ggsci
   GGSCI> encrypt password ogg blowfish
   ```

   The output of the preceding command will be as follows:

   ```
   No key specified, using default key...


   Encrypted password:   AACAAAAAAAAAAADAHBLDCCIIOIRFNEPB


   Algorithm used:   BLOWFISH
   ```

2. Open the Extract parameter file as follows:

   ```
   $ ./ggsci
   GGSCI> edit param ext01sand
   ```

   Change the following line in the file:

   ```
   USERID ogg, PASSWORD ogg
   ```

   to:

   ```
   USERID ogg, PASSWORD AACAAAAAAAAAAADAHBLDCCIIOIRFNEPB, &
   ENCRYPTKEY DEFAULT
   ```

3. Stop and start the Extract so that the encryption key is read in:

   ```
   $ ./ggsci
   GGSCI> stop ext01sand
   GGSCI> start ext01sand
   ```

   To complete the cycle, you should repeat the preceding steps at your target environments as well.

4. Now we would be encrypting the trail files. Stop your Extract/Replicat using the following commands:

   ```
   GGSCI> stop e*
   GGSCI> stop r*
   GGSCI> edit param ex01sand
   ```

Add `ENCRYPTTRAIL` just before the following line:

```
EXTTRAIL /u01/app/oracle/gg/dirdat/pr
```

After adding the preceding line , it should now look like the following in your parameter file:

```
ENCRYPTTRAIL
EXTTRAIL /u01/app/oracle/gg/dirdat/pr
```

Save the file and exit.

5. Follow the preceding steps to enable the replicat to decrypt the trail files before they are read for processing:

    ```
    GGSCI> edit param re01sand
    ```

    Scroll down the editor and just before your `MAP` commands add the following line:

    ```
    DECRYPTTRAIL
    ```

    Save the file and exit as follows:

    ```
    GGSCI> start e*

    GGSCI> start r*
    ```

    You must now repeat these steps on your target server as well.

The steps for **Transparent Data Encryption** (**TDE**) and OGG Instructions are as follows (informational):

1. Install Oracle patch 9409423 on top of Oracle 11.1.0.7.

2. Installing Oracle patch 9409423 to your Oracle database is beyond the scope of this book. Please consult with your DBA or Oracle documentation.

3. Run the following command after the patch is installed:

    ```
    $ sqlplus / as sysdba

    SQL> @$ORACLE_HOME/rdbms/admin/prvtclkm.plb
    ```

4. Install Oracle patch 10395645 on top of Oracle 10.2.0.5, 11.1.0.7, and 11.2.0.2.

5. Once the TDE is configured correctly and operational, OGG can now read Oracle's encrypted data.

> For Oracle versions 10.2.0.5, 11.1.0.7, and 11.2.0.2
>
> Installing Oracle patch 103956445 on top of Oracle versions 10.2.0.5, 11.1.0.7, and 11.2.0.2 is beyond the scope of this book. Please consult with your DBA or Oracle documentation.

6. Once the TDE is configured by your DBA, you can now deploy OGG encryption as stated in the preceding steps.

How it works...

Encrypting the OGG database user is quite trivial as shown in the preceding section, but generally the Blowfish algorithm is quite weak. OGG allows you to also use **Advanced Encryption Standard** (**AES**) algorithms for 128, 192, and 256 bits. Using AES ciphers needs the use of an ENCKEYS file.

Once you've encrypted the database user ID, you no longer need to paste it in your parameter file. However, make sure you recall the clear text password and place it in an electronic lock box so that you can recall the original password should you ever forget it.

Encrypting OGG trail files is just as easy as using the keyword ENCRYPTTRAIL on the source server so that the trail files are scrambled when written to disk and are not human-readable. On the target server, the Replicat processes need to decrypt the trail files in order to process them by means of the keyword DECRYPTTRAIL. If the replicat does not have the keyword DECRYPTTRAIL, the process will abend and it will not start until you add the keyword in the replicat's parameter file.

Managing Oracle GoldenGate (Simple)

So far we've talked mostly about configurations and very little about managing an OGG instance. We'll discuss some of the more common management commands you'll probably use most often.

How to do it...

Here you'll get to know some of the most useful commands for displaying OGG status and/or for root cause analysis investigation.

1. We would be investigating long-running transactions when there is a sequence lag of 1 or more logs difference between the recovery checkpoint and the current checkpoint. We do it using the following command:

   ```
   GGSCI> info ex01sand showch
   ```

The output of the preceding command will be as follows:

...

```
Recovery Checkpoint (position of oldest unprocessed transaction in
the data source):
    Thread #: 1
    Sequence #: 10501    ß way behind by 20 logs
    ...


Current Checkpoint (position of last record read in the data
source):
    Thread #: 1
    Sequence #: 10521

    ...
```

You or your database administrator would need to troubleshoot as to which transaction is not committing its work. You might need to wait for the transaction to complete; or sometimes the user of that transaction might have forgotten to commit its work and you need to alert him/her to either commit their work or roll it back to clear the long-running transaction lag.

2. We can check Extract/Replicat status' for a running instance using the following command.

```
GGSCI> send pp01sand status
```

The output of the preceding command will be as follows:

```
EXTRACT PP01SAND (PID 696398)
    Current status: Recovery complete: At EOF

    Current read position:
    Sequence #: 11
    RBA: 1096
    Timestamp: 2012-12-17 11:05:44.778119
    Extract Trail: /u01/app/oracle/gg/dirdat/pr

    Current write position:
    Sequence #: 6
    RBA: 1408
    Timestamp: 2012-12-17 11:20:03.446074
    Extract Trail: /u01/app/oracle/goldengate/dirdat/rp
```

3. For measuring the true lag between the data source and Extract process use the following command:

GGSCI> send * getlag

The output of the preceding command will be as follows:

```
Sending GETLAG request to EXTRACT EX01SAND ...
Last record lag: 1 seconds.
At EOF, no more records to process.
...
```

However, the following command is more common:

GGSCI> info all

The output of the preceding command will be as follows:

Program	Status	Group	Lag at Chkpt	Time Since Chkpt
MANAGER	RUNNING			
EXTRACT	RUNNING	EX01SAND	00:00:00	00:00:09
EXTRACT	RUNNING	PP01SAND	00:00:00	00:00:06
REPLICAT	RUNNING	RE01SAND	00:00:00	00:00:05

4. The Miscellaneous commands used are as follows. This closes the current trail file and opens a new one:

GGSCI> send pp01sand rollover

GGSCI> send ex01sand stop

GGSCI> send ext01sand forcestop

When an extract does not stop normally, you can abruptly stop it with the `forcestop` option.

5. Following are the different ways to report stats on objects (tables):

GGSCI> stats ex01sand latest table scott.*

The output of the preceding command will be as follows:

```
Extracting from SCOTT.TCUSTMER to SCOTT.TCUSTMER:

*** Latest statistics since 2012-12-17 12:57:36 ***
        Total inserts                          0.00
        Total updates                          0.00
        Total deletes                          1.00
```

```
            Total discards                          0.00
            Total operations                        1.00

End of Statistics.
```

6. Reporting the status as a rate of insert/update/deletes per time interval is done using the following commands:

    ```
    GGSCI> stats ex01sand table.tcustmer reportrate sec|min|hr

    GGSCI> stats ex01sand totalsonly scott.*
    ```

7. For killing a Replicat / Deleting an E/R group, use the following command:

    ```
    GGSCI> kill replicat <group>

    GGSCI> delete <group> [!]
    ```

8. The trail commands to be used are as follows. When you add trails to your extracts, you can specify the size of the trails with the keyword **megabytes n** where n is a number representing the size in megabytes.

    ```
    GGSCI> add exttrail | rmttrail, extract <group name> megabytes n

    GGSCI> alter exttrail | rmttrail extract <group name> megabytes n

    GGSCI> delete exttrail | rmttrail <trail name>
    ```

How it works...

Long running transactions (**LRT**) are identified by OGG via the WARNLONGTRANS parameter which by default is 60 minutes and it checks after every 5 minutes. It is wise to set this in your extract parameter file to a valid value for your environment. When checking for an LRT with the show checkpoint showch option to the info command, you ideally want the sequence number for both the recovery and current checkpoint to be the same; under normal circumstances this will be the case. But if the difference is more than 1 sequence, then you need to investigate further as to which transaction is holding up the delay. An LRT is not a true lag because it is still processing rows, but just not committing until the end of the transaction. The SQL may be a bad design so it's worth investigating and identifying the DML in question and suggesting a more scalable approach to the designer. OGG has a monitoring tool called the Director which normally will alert you of such LRT and will also identify the long-running transaction automatically.

The info <group name> detail command will give you detailed information regarding your environment. Try it, and usually I save the output along with info * showch to a Notepad file for later reference should it be needed for troubleshooting. I normally perform this when I make structural changes to tables or add/remove tables from the OGG configuration.

Checking for lags is a common command used by DBA's as a quick way to detect any lags with the E/R or both with the `info all` command. If the lag is in the range of several minutes to hours, you need to investigate further. It could be due to an LRT, network latencies, or a number of other issues with your database performance. There are times it is obvious, but other times you really need to dig in through OGG logs and/or database logs. This one time, I had a huge lag with the data pump and the `send <group name> status` command helped me identify that the issue was related outside the OGG/database. The issue was with network latencies. The command output will display the current read position in the local trail file directory and the current write position to the remote trail. The current read position has a sequence number associated; say 11 as in our case in the preceding example, which is part of the trail file name. An example of a directory listing of the trail files is as follows:

```
-rw-rw-rw-   1 oracle   oinstall        1096 Dec 17 11:05 pr000010
-rw-rw-rw-   1 oracle   oinstall        1231 Dec 17 12:57 pr000011
...
-rw-rw-rw-   1 oracle   oinstall        1231 Dec 17 13:40 pr000030
```

So, the pump is not shipping the trails as fast as they should and we seem to be 29 trail files behind. At this point you need to focus on probable network latencies by contacting your network administrator and working with him/her.

The `...getlag` command is also a very useful command when you stop the extract and want to ensure the pump and replicat have a chance to drain all its processing while they are still running and have no more records to process. Equally, you can also issue the following command to either the pump or replicat while the extract is stopped to check for any further processing by either:

```
GGSCI> send PP01SAND logend
```

The output of the preceding command will be as follows:

```
Sending LOGEND request to EXTRACT PP01SAND ...
YES.
```

`YES` meaning that all the records have been processed in the data source and there aren't any further records to process.

Finally, you can check out some of the stats commands to display statistics about your objects. Try them in your environment.

Performance tuning (Simple)

In this last installment we'll examine some of the aspects that may help you to derive better throughput in your OGG processing.

How to do it...

One of the challenges of performance tuning is in deciding which component of Oracle GoldenGate environment needs tuning. In the following section you'll find a number of tips in order to improve OGG processing:

1. When source and target have identical data structures and character set, add the following to your extract or data pump:

    ```
    PASSTHRU
    ```

2. To scale up similar DML activity in your Replicat processes when the applier is underperforming, add the following keyword in your replicat parameter file:

    ```
    BATCHSQL
    ```

3. Speeding up Replicat processing since we don't wait for the commit marker is done as follows:

    ```
    SQLEXEC "ALTER SESSION SET COMMIT_WRITE  = NOWAIT"
    ```

4. For improving network throughput when shipping trail files across the network to your target server; please refer to the recipe *Implementing design considerations (Simple)* for buffer sizing calculations.

    ```
    RMTHOST hostb MGRPORT 7820 TCPBUFSIZE 10000000
    ```

5. We will be implementing parallel data pumps and corresponding parallel Replicats to speed up throughput along the wire.

    Sample parameter file for your first pump at source server is as follows:

    ```
    EXTRACT pp01HR

    PASSTHRU

    RMTHOST hostb MGRPORT 7820
    RMTTRAIL /u01/app/oracle/goldengate/dirdat/HA

    DISCARDFILE /u01/app/oracle/gg/dirrpt/pp01hr.dsc, APPEND
    ```

```
-- Tables for transport

TABLE    HR.EMPLOYEE ;
TABLE    HR.JOBS ;
```

Sample parameter file for your second pump at source server is as follows:

```
EXTRACT pp02HR

PASSTHRU

RMTHOST hostb MGRPORT 7820
RMTTRAIL /u01/app/oracle/goldengate/dirdat/HB

DISCARDFILE /u01/app/oracle/gg/dirrpt/pp02hr.dsc, APPEND

-- Tables for transport

TABLE    HR.LOCATION ;
TABLE    HR.COUNTRY ;
TABLE    HR.REGION ;
```

Sample corresponding replicat parameter for the first pump at target server is as follows:

```
REPLICAT re01hr

SETENV (ORACLE_SID="TRG101")
SETENV (ORACLE_HOME="/u01/app/oracle/product/11.1.0/db_1")
SETENV (NLS_LANG = "AMERICAN_AMERICA.AL32UTF8")

USERID ogg PASSWORD ogg

DISCARDFILE /u01/app/oracle/goldengate/dirrpt/re01hr.dsc, APPEND
DISCARDROLLOVER at 01:00

ReportCount Every 30 Minutes, Rate
REPORTROLLOVER at 01:30

DBOPTIONS DEFERREFCONST
ASSUMETARGETDEFS

MAP HR.EMPLOYEE , TARGET HR.EMPLOYEE ;
MAP HR.JOBS     , TARGET HR.JOBS     ;
```

Sample corresponding replicat parameter for the second pump at target server is as follows:

```
REPLICAT re02hr

SETENV (ORACLE_SID="TRG101")
SETENV (ORACLE_HOME="/u01/app/oracle/product/11.1.0/db_1")
SETENV (NLS_LANG = "AMERICAN_AMERICA.AL32UTF8")

USERID ogg PASSWORD ogg

DISCARDFILE /u01/app/oracle/goldengate/dirrpt/re02hr.dsc, APPEND
DISCARDROLLOVER at 01:00

ReportCount Every 30 Minutes, Rate
REPORTROLLOVER at 01:30

DBOPTIONS DEFERREFCONST
ASSUMETARGETDEFS

MAP HR.LOCATION , TARGET HR.LOCATION ;
MAP HR.COUNTRY  , TARGET HR.COUNTRY  ;
MAP HR. REGION  , TARGET HR.REGION   ;
```

6. We would now be splitting a single table's workload to enhance throughput of large and heavily accessed tables.

   For splitting the HISTORY table in 3 ranges at source server perform the following:

```
RMTTRAIL /u01/app/oracle/GG/aa
TABLE HR.HISTORY, FILTER (@RANGE(1, 3)) ;

RMTTRAIL /u01/app/oracle/GG/ab
TABLE HR.HISTORY, FILTER (@RANGE(2, 3)) ;

RMTTRAIL /u01/app/oracle/GG/ac
TABLE HR.HISTORY, FILTER (@RANGE(3, 3)) ;
```

Corresponding `HISTORY` table ranges on the target server are as follows:

```
EXTRAIL /u01/app/oracle/GG/aa
MAP HR.HISTORY , TARGET HR.HISTORY, FILTER (@RANGE(1,3));


EXTRAIL /u01/app/oracle/GG/ab
MAP HR.HISTORY , TARGET HR.HISTORY, FILTER (@RANGE(2,3));


EXTRAIL /u01/app/oracle/GG/ac
MAP HR.HISTORY , TARGET HR.HISTORY, FILTER (@RANGE(3,3));
```

How it works...

When you use `PASSTHRU` in your data pump, the benefit is that the extract does not have to lookup table definitions either from the database or from data definition files. The data pump process instead handles reading and sending the local trail files over to the target system.

Use `BATCHSQL` in your Replicat parameter file to organize similar SQL statements into arrays and to apply them into an accelerated rate.

The `commit_rate=nowait` command speeds up Replicat processing. The parameter alters the Replicat Oracle session to not wait for commits. Similar to an asynchronous state, however, the transaction is persisted through the redo.

Using the `@RANGE` function is a powerful way to increase a heavily used table's throughput. It divides the rows of any table across two or more OGG processes. In our example we have split the range in 3; for example, `FILTER @RANGE(1,3)`, `FILTER @RANGE(2,3)`. The `@RANGE` is safe and scalable to use. It preserves data integrity by ensuring that the same row is always processed by the same process group.

If you like to use a specific column as the range to split on, the syntax is as follows:

```
MAP HR.HISTORY , TARGET HR.HISTORY, FILTER (@RANGE(1,3, ID));
MAP HR.HISTORY , TARGET HR.HISTORY, FILTER (@RANGE(2,3, ID));
MAP HR.HISTORY , TARGET HR.HISTORY, FILTER (@RANGE(3,3, ID));
```

Since any column can be specified for this function, any related table with referential integrity must be grouped together into the same process or trail to preserve referential integrity.

`@RANGE` computes a hash value of the `KEYCOLS` of the `TABLE` or `MAP` statement if one is used. Otherwise, the primary key will be used.

Using the Extract to calculate the ranges is far more efficient than using the Replicat. Calculating ranges at the target requires the Replicat to read through the entire trail to find the data that meets the range specification.

About Packt Publishing

Packt, pronounced 'packed', published its first book "*Mastering phpMyAdmin for Effective MySQL Management*" in April 2004 and subsequently continued to specialize in publishing highly focused books on specific technologies and solutions.

Our books and publications share the experiences of your fellow IT professionals in adapting and customizing today's systems, applications, and frameworks. Our solution based books give you the knowledge and power to customize the software and technologies you're using to get the job done. Packt books are more specific and less general than the IT books you have seen in the past. Our unique business model allows us to bring you more focused information, giving you more of what you need to know, and less of what you don't.

Packt is a modern, yet unique publishing company, which focuses on producing quality, cutting-edge books for communities of developers, administrators, and newbies alike. For more information, please visit our website: www.packtpub.com.

Writing for Packt

We welcome all inquiries from people who are interested in authoring. Book proposals should be sent to author@packtpub.com. If your book idea is still at an early stage and you would like to discuss it first before writing a formal book proposal, contact us; one of our commissioning editors will get in touch with you.

We're not just looking for published authors; if you have strong technical skills but no writing experience, our experienced editors can help you develop a writing career, or simply get some additional reward for your expertise.

Oracle 11g Anti-hacker's Cookbook

ISBN: 978-1-849685-26-9   Paperback: 302 pages

Over 50 recipes and scenarios to hack, defend, and secure your Oracle Database

1. Learn to protect your sensitive data by using industry certified techniques

2. Implement and use ultimate techniques in Oracle Security and new security features introduced in Oracle 11g R2

3. Implement strong network communication security using different encryption solutions provided by Oracle Advanced Security

Oracle Database XE 11gR2 Jump Start Guide

ISBN: 978-1-849686-74-7   Paperback: 146 pages

Build and manage your Oracle Database 11g XE environment with this fast paced, practical guide

1. Install and configure Oracle Database XE on Windows and Linux

2. Develop database applications using Oracle Application Express

3. Back up, restore, and tune your database

4. Includes clear step-by-step instructions and examples

Please check **www.PacktPub.com** for information on our titles